Center Brent Sutter

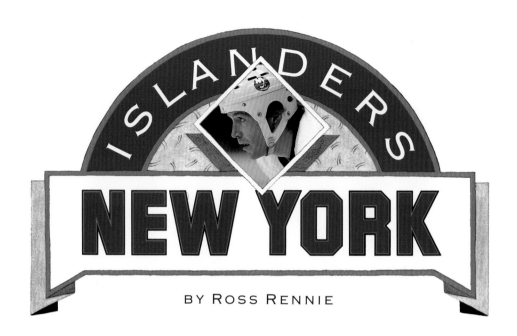

ISLANDERS

NEW YORK

BY ROSS RENNIE

CREATIVE EDUCATION INC.

Published by Creative Education, Inc.
123 S. Broad Street, Mankato, Minnesota 56001

Designed by Rita Marshall
Photos by Bruce Bennett Studios,
Frank Howard/Protography and Wide World Photos

Library of Congress Cataloging-in-Publication Data

Rennie, Ross.
   The New York Islanders/by Ross Rennie.
   p.   cm.
   Summary: A history of the New York metropolitan area's younger
National Hockey League team, the New York Islanders.
   ISBN 0-88682-284-X
   1. New York Islanders (Hockey team)—History—Juvenile literature.
[1. New York Islanders (Hockey team)—History.   2. Hockey—History.]
I. Title.
GV848.N4R46   1989
796.96'264'09747245—dc20   89-37735
                                                             CIP
                                                             AC

THE BEGINNINGS: 1972–1974

New York City is known throughout the United States as the Big Apple, the metropolis where the people are more colorful, the buildings are higher, and the sites are grander than they appear to be in the rest of the nation. Everything is larger than life, including the city's professional sports teams. This is the home of the famed Brooklyn Dodgers, the infamous Yankees, the amazing Mets, the Super Bowl champion Jets, and the venerable hockey club, the New York Rangers. It is also the home of the New York Islanders, a club that captivated the hockey world by establishing a dynasty in the National Hockey League in its first decade of existence. This is their story.

Left wing Bob Bourne was a superb penalty killer.

The New York Islanders were one of two expansion teams to join the NHL.

In 1966 it was decided that the time had come for expansion in the NHL. The league would grow from six to twelve teams for the 1967–68 season, with the new teams forming in St. Louis, Pittsburgh, Oakland, Los Angeles, Minnesota, and Philadelphia. In 1970 Buffalo and Vancouver were also added to the league. The instant success of these franchises inspired the NHL governors to add more teams.

The league announced that two new teams would be welcomed for the 1972–73 season, the Atlanta Flames and the New York Islanders. The NHL was taking a gamble, hoping that the New York metropolitan area could support a second NHL team.

The prospect didn't bother Roy Boe, who, along with nineteen other partners, purchased the Long Island franchise on December 30, 1971.

Once the deal was finalized, Boe began his first recruitment plan. The goal was to find a general manager with the qualities of intelligence, patience, and humor.

On February 15, 1972, Boe announced his choice of William Arthur ("Bill") Torrey, a thirty-seven-year-old native of Montreal who was born across the street from the Montreal Forum. Torrey had been business manager and public relations director of the Pittsburgh Hornets in the American Hockey League. He had also spent two years with the California (Oakland) Seals. In which time he helped lift the Seals from last place in the West Division in 1967–68 to play-off berths the following two seasons.

With the job of organizing a team before him, Torrey's prospects for finding first-rate players were exceptionally dim. He knew what he wanted, however, and he had a clear three to five-year plan for building a winning team.

Goalie Glenn Resch recorded twenty-five shutouts during his career with the Islanders.

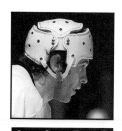

Billy Harris was an original member of the Islanders' first-year team.

A milestone in the Islanders' young life was reached in June 1972 when the expansion draft enabled them to stock their roster with experienced players. By far the best-known Islander pick was Eddie Westfall, a superb defensive forward who had played for the Boston Bruins' Stanley Cup championship teams in 1970 and again in 1972.

The Islanders made another meaningful move when they signed their second and third amateur draft choices, center Lorne Henning and right wing Bob Nystrom.

Finding an adequate coach was another story. Torrey finally selected thirty-eight-year-old veteran NHL center Phil Goyette. To say that he had a difficult task would be an understatement. Even Torrey admitted that.

New York's first game would prove Torrey right. A crowd of 12,221 turned out on opening night, October 7, 1972, to see the Islanders defeated by the Flames by a score of 3–2.

Although coach Goyette maintained an optimistic front, the on-ice results were less than encouraging. As may have been expected, the Islanders' play left much to be desired in their first year in the league. Naturally, their record reflected their youth and inexperience. Even though the team made a coaching change in January, naming Earl Ingarfield to replace Goyette, the season was still a disaster.

When the won-lost record was compiled at season's end it showed that the Islanders had captured only twelve games, a record low, and lost sixty, a record high. They had finished seventy-two points behind their crosstown rivals the Rangers.

But on the good side, the finish guaranteed them the first pick in the amateur draft. That meant that Torrey had a better than fair chance of signing nineteen-year-old Denis Potvin, a defenseman with the Ottawa 67s who had broken all of Bobby Orr's junior scoring records.

To ensure the acquisition of Potvin, Torrey swung a late-season deal with the Philadelphia Flyers and obtained Denis's older brother, Jean Potvin. The Islanders knew that more than anything, Denis wanted to play alongside his brother. And they were right.

Jean Potvin was acquired by the Islanders to ensure the signing of his younger brother, Denis.

The six-foot, 205-pound Potvin arrived with a reputation that almost overshadowed the one preceding Orr's arrival on the NHL scene. Denis was tough and, unlike Orr, liked to hit the enemy as much as he liked to score goals.

Potvin needed a coach who would stress the defensive fundamentals that might have eluded him in the junior ranks. When Ingarfield asked to be relieved of the coaching job, Bill Torrey offered the assignment to Al Arbour, who had long been considered the "defenseman's defenseman" when he skated for the Chicago Blackhawks, Toronto Maple Leafs, and St. Louis Blues.

Under the guidance of Arbour, Denis completed the 1973–74 season with seventeen goals and thirty-seven assists for fifty-four points. He won the Calder Memorial Trophy as "the player selected as the most proficient in his first year of competition in the National Hockey League," otherwise known as the rookie of the year.

Although Potvin was the major headline-grabber among the Islanders' defense, there were others who helped strengthen the group in the club's second season. Torrey

Denis Potvin won rookie of the year honors in 1974. (pages 10–11)

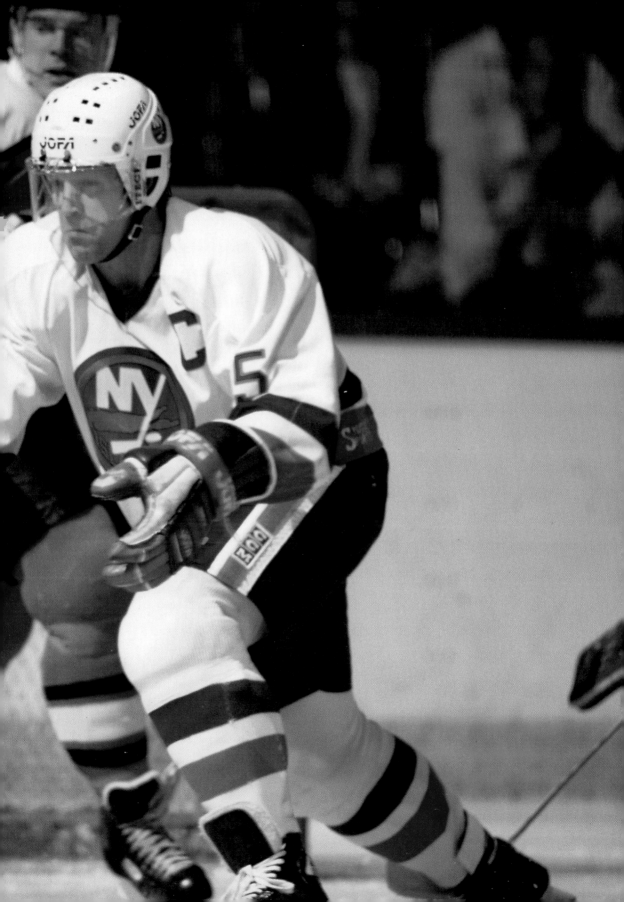

picked up twenty-nine-year-old Bert Marshall in the June 1973 draft, and he added youngster Dave Lewis and Gerry Hart to go along with the Potvin brothers.

Despite the Potvins and the team's improved performance in the 1973–74 season, the Islanders' final results showed a 19-41-18 won, lost, and tied record, putting them in last place again in the East Division.

A GLIMPSE OF THE FUTURE: 1975–1978

The Islanders began the 1974–75 season with high hopes. They opened at the Montreal Forum and extended Les Canadiens to a 5–5 tie. Even more impressive was the 5–3 lead the Islanders held over Montreal with less than two minutes remaining before allowing the Canadiens to tie the game.

By the end of October, they were in first place. It was clear that the managerial-coaching team of Torrey and Arbour was blending very well. The proof was in the standings. Although they didn't stay league leaders, the Islanders had definitely established themselves as a play-off threat for the first time in their brief NHL life.

Torrey still wanted more power up front and he went to the NHL marketplace in search of scorers. He made a trade with the Minnesota North Stars, acquiring forwards J. P. Parise and Jude Drouin in exchange for Ernie Hicke, Doug Rombough and Craig Cameron, three marginal forwards.

With added scoring power the Islanders qualified for the play-offs that season, advancing all the way to the semi-finals before being stopped by the Philadelphia Flyers. It took the Flyers, the defending Stanley Cup champions, seven games to defeat the Islanders. For the young club, it was a glimpse into their future.

In the 1975–76 season, the Islanders continued to improve. They finished in second place in the Patrick Division, nineteen points ahead of the third-place Atlanta Flames. The Islanders were matched against the Vancouver Canucks in the first round and quickly eliminated them in two games, 5–3 and 3–1.

Next came the Buffalo Sabres, a team that had given the Islanders trouble during the season. The Sabres easily won the opening game 5–3 and then beat New York 3–2

1 9 7 5

Coach Al Arbour guided his team to the semi-finals in the Islanders' first play-off appearance.

*Denis Potvin won
his first of three
James Norris
Memorial Trophies
as the NHL's Most
Valuable
Defenseman.*

to take a two-games-to-none lead. The Islanders, however, responded with four straight wins to eliminate the Sabres. They had impressed the Sabres with their effort.

"I think the Islanders wanted it more than we did" said Sabre defenseman Jerry Korab.

The Islanders lost their next series to the tough Montreal Canadiens, but they were the only team to give Montreal any trouble during the play-offs. Al Arbour's squad came close to winning both the first and second games at the Forum before bowing out in five games.

"Believe me," said Montreal goalie Ken Dryden, "they are going to be as good—or better—in years to come."

Over the next three seasons, the Islanders continued their strong play. They consistently finished at or near the top of the league, compiling at least forty-seven wins each season.

Denis Potvin became the league's premier defenseman, combining effective defensive skill with a potent offensive attack. He captained the Islanders' extremely productive power play and was the only defenseman other than Bobby Orr to score more than thirty goals in a season. To cap off his accomplishments, Denis was awarded the Norris Trophy three times as the NHL's most valuable defenseman.

Along with Potvin, the Islanders were also led by two other standout players, Bryan Trottier and Mike Bossy. Trottier was known as both an outstanding playmaker and a prolific scorer. He was acknowledged as the best all-purpose center in the league, capable of issuing fierce body checks when necessary. Bryan emerged as the NHL's scoring champion in the 1979 season and also won the most valuable player award.

Bryan Trottier was an adroit playmaker and a masterful scorer.

The talented Mike Bossy (right) joined Bryan Trottier (page 17) to form a fierce scoring duo.

Bossy, the Islanders all-time scoring leader, had an amazingly accurate, quickly released shot that opponents found nearly impossible to defense against. Besides displaying incredible scoring skills, Bossy also was a three-time recipient of the Lady Byng Memorial Trophy, awarded on the basis of sportsmanship and playing ability.

The talents of these three players and their teammates gave the Islanders a spectacular regular season in 1978–79.

They were the best team in the league with a 51-15-14 record for 116 points, one better than the Montreal Canadiens. Bossy, Trottier and Potvin had all scored more than

Opponents found it nearly impossible to stop Mike Bossy.

A menacing checker, Clark Gilles complemented linemates Bossy and Trottier perfectly.

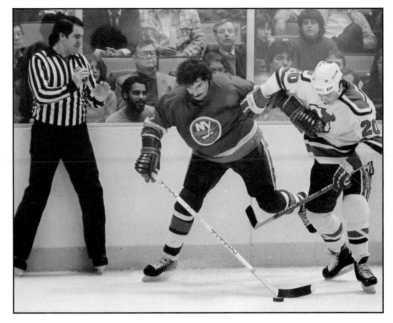

one hundred points. If there ever was a year in which the Islanders were finally going to reach the Stanley Cup finals, 1978–79 seemed to be it.

The playoffs started well enough as the Islanders eliminated the Chicago Blackhawks in four straight games.

Next came their old rivals, the New York Rangers, who had eliminated the Los Angeles Kings and the Philadelphia Flyers and who were playing inspired hockey.

The series was a classic as the two teams battled mightily. At the end of three games, the Rangers led the series by a 2–1 margin.

In game four, the score was tied 2–2 after three periods and overtime was necessary. Nearly four minutes into the session, the puck squirted into the Ranger end of the ice and it became a race between Ranger goalie John Davidson and Islander Bob Nystrom to see who would get to it first. They both got there at the same time and the puck popped up into the air. When the puck finally came down Nystrom was able to knock it into the open net and the Islanders had tied the series.

In game five at Nassau Coliseum, the Rangers prevailed as Anders Hedberg scored a late goal for the 4–3 win.

In game six, the Rangers ended the Islanders' dream by winning 2–1 to capture the series.

1 9 7 9

Bryan Trottier was the NHL's most valuable player as well as scoring champion.

The secret to the Rangers' success was their ability to shut down the Islanders' best scoring line of Bossy, Trottier and Clark Gillies. The group was held to very few points in the series.

Once again, the Islanders ended a season in disappointing fashion.

One scene told the story for the Islanders. As the Rangers celebrated on the Madison Square Garden ice, Islanders' captain Denis Potvin sat motionless and stunned on the players bench, his head resting on the plexiglass behind the bench. The Islanders would have to wait another year.

THE CHAMPIONSHIP YEARS: 1979–1983

In spite of all their talent, the Islanders did not play impressively during the 1979–80 season. Al Arbour was upset with the team as they stayed at or near the .500 mark for most of the year. The Islanders continued to struggle until they made a move that turned their season around. In March they traded Billy Harris and Dave Lewis to the Los Angeles Kings for Butch Goring.

Butch brought a new attitude to the Islanders. "I think we can win the Stanley Cup," said Goring just days after the trade. "I don't see why we can't be the best team in hockey this year."

The Islanders also added Olympic defenseman Ken Morrow to help shore up the back line.

These two moves, particularly the Goring trade, led the Islanders to a furious finish in which they won their last twelve games. They entered the play-offs full of confidence.

1 9 8 0

The Islanders won the Stanley Cup in Denis Potvin's first season as team captain.

New York easily defeated their first round play-off opponents, the Los Angeles Kings, and went on to face the Boston Bruins in the next round. The Islanders outlasted the Bruins in a five-game series; many Islanders saw that series as a turning point for the team.

"After beating Boston, we never looked back," said Bobby Nystrom. "Other teams thought they could intimidate us, like Toronto did in '78. But we stood together and backed each other to the fullest."

The semifinals matched the Islanders against the Buffalo Sabres. The Sabres had finished the season with the second-best record in the NHL under coach Scotty Bowman.

Despite their stellar season, the Sabres were unable to overcome the tough Islander forechecking, specialty unit play, and overall balance. The Islanders won the series in seven games.

The effect of Butch Goring on the team was noticeable. "Butchie could light a fire under anyone," said coach Arbour. "He's a winner and he works hard to make everyone else feel like winners."

Inspired by Goring, the New York Islanders suddenly found themselves in the Stanley Cup finals, battling the

Butch Goring was the sparkplug behind the Islanders' first Stanley Cup victory.

(clockwise): Bobby Nystrom, Ken Morrow, Brent Sutter, Tomas Jonsson.

Philadelphia Flyers. Although the Islanders were not favored to win, the combination of their tenacious defense and explosive scoring attack was too much for the Flyers. The Islanders defeated Philadelphia in six games to win their first Stanley Cup.

The winning point came on an overtime goal by Bob Nystrom. "That was the greatest thrill, something that you can never describe in words," Nystrom said.

For Al Arbour and Bill Torrey, it was the culmination of many years of hard work.

Although known as a defensive forward, John Tonelli scored five goals in a game against Toronto.

"When I started out here, I dreamed of a day when the Stanley Cup would be ours," said Torrey. "When it actually happens, everything in the past doesn't seem to matter. Getting there makes it all worthwhile."

Many teams win league championships one year only to begin a decline the following season. With the competition found in the NHL it is difficult to sustain the level of play necessary to retain Lord Stanley's Cup for more than one year. However, the New York Islanders were not an ordinary championship club. With their Stanley Cup victory in the 1979–80 season, the team embarked on a era of dominance in the NHL that would see the Islanders win four straight league championships.

Led by the brilliant trio of Potvin, Bossy, and Trottier, the club was virtually impossible to stop. The talk around the league turned to the word dynasty. "We have the elements to be a dynasty," said Mike Bossy, the most valuable player in the 1981–82 play-offs. "But I don't want guys getting satisfied. I want to keep winning the Cup."

Backing up the splendid play of Potvin, Bossy and Trottier were the solid defense of Ken Morrow and the outstanding goaltending of Billy Smith. Morrow, a member of

The flawless goaltending of Billy Smith, (pages 26–27) was a key to the Islanders championship victories.

1 9 8 2

Billy Smith was awarded the Vezina Trophy as the league's most valuable goaltender.

the 1980 U.S. Olympic hockey team, became the only hockey player ever to win an Olympic gold medal and the Stanley Cup in the same year. His consistent defensive play was a big factor in the Islanders' championship victories.

After their fourth Stanley Cup win, Morrow commented, "I never saw a team so intent on winning as this one was in the play-offs."

Perhaps the most committed was the Islanders' goaltender. Many consider Billy Smith the key reason for the Islanders' amazing string of NHL championships. Smith, one of the original members of the franchise, played goal for the club during each of their Stanley Cup victories. Winner of both the Conn Smythe and Vezina trophies, Smith's stellar performances in the nets stymied the Islanders' adversaries.

At least one of his opponents credited Smith with a large part of his team's incredible success. "I remember when the Islanders beat us four straight," said Wayne Gretzky of the 1983 finals, when New York's opponent was Gretzky's team at that time, the Edmonton Oilers. "We were playing tremendous hockey through the first three rounds. We went into the Northlands and really dominated that game, but Billy Smith shut us down. We got beat, 2–0, with an empty net goal, and they won the series four straight."

As magnificent as the Islander championship seasons were, the era eventually came to an end. Although the team won fifty games during the 1983–84 season and advanced to the Stanley Cup finals, they had to battle the Edmonton Oilers, the team of the future, for the NHL championship. Injuries, fatigue, and the tough play of Edmonton signaled the end of the Islander championship reign.

When the Oilers won the Stanley Cup that season, it was the first play-off series since 1979 that the Islanders had lost—an amazing nineteen straight series wins. It was time for the Islanders to look toward the future.

TODAY'S NEW YORK ISLANDERS: 1984 AND BEYOND

1 9 8 3

Pat LaFontaine, known for his phenomenal scoring ability, was drafted as the Islanders' first pick.

The Islanders continued to record respectable seasons throughout the 1980s. Although not able to match their championship era of the early 1980s, the team qualified for the play-offs every season and advanced to the Stanley Cup finals in the 1986–87 season.

With their former team leaders aging and beginning to retire, the club was clearly in a rebuilding stage. The team introduced rookie Kelly Hrudey as the goaltender of the future. Other young players such as Gord Dineen and Mikko Makela began to make their presence felt.

Another addition, Pat LaFontaine, would soon make a major impact on the club. LaFontaine grew up in a suburb of Detroit. His father, John, an executive with Chrysler, was Pat's Pee Wee league coach. Father and son practiced often on the frozen lake behind their home; when the lake didn't freeze, John would improvise by flooding a rink in their backyard.

Pat excelled at hockey at an early age. After scoring an

The fine play of Pat LaFontaine inspired comparisons to Trottier and Bossy.

Forward Mikko Makela showed definite all-star potential.   31

incredible 175 goals in just seventy-nine games for his midget team, he decided to leave home to play in the Canadian junior league.

After playing with the U.S. Olympic hockey team in 1984, LaFontaine was drafted by the Islanders. Throughout his career with the club, the speedy forward has scored more goals with each successive season and ranks among team leaders in both goals and assists. The Islander fans began to compare his performances with those of Trottier and Bossy in their prime.

Along with the new faces on the team such as La-Fontaine, an era came to a close in 1986 when veteran coach Al Arbour decided to resign after thirteen years on the job. The highly respected Arbour had more wins than all but two other coaches in league history, with 594 regular-season victories; his 113 play-off victories left him just one shy of Scotty Bowman's all-time record. More importantly, he was the general who guided the once-ragtag Islanders to four Stanley Cups.

"I've had a good run at it," said Arbour at his resignation press conference. "It's time to let somebody else take the reins. The team needs a fresh approach."

Although Arbour's departure left a definite void, his replacement, Terry Simpson, compiled a winning season each year at the helm of the Islanders. As the team enters the 1990s, they continue to build on their talented young squad, hoping that general manager Bill Torrey once again will be the architect of a dynasty.

1 9 8 4

Patrick Flatley set a club rookie scoring record by notching fifteen points in the play-offs.